Home, Sweet Home

To Stefan and Roland, with love from Caroline

Copyright © QEB Publishing, Inc. 2008

Published in the United States by
QEB Publishing, Inc.
23062 La Cadena Drive
Laguna Hills, CA 92653

www.qeb-publishing.com

A CIP record for this book is available from the Library of Congress.

ISBN 978 1 59566 910 0

Author Caroline Pitcher
Illustrator Jenny Arthur
Editor Clare Weaver
Designer Alix Wood
Consultant Anne Faundez

Publisher Steve Evans
Creative Director Zeta Davies

Printed and bound in China

Home, Sweet Home

Caroline Pitcher

Illustrated by Jenny Arthur

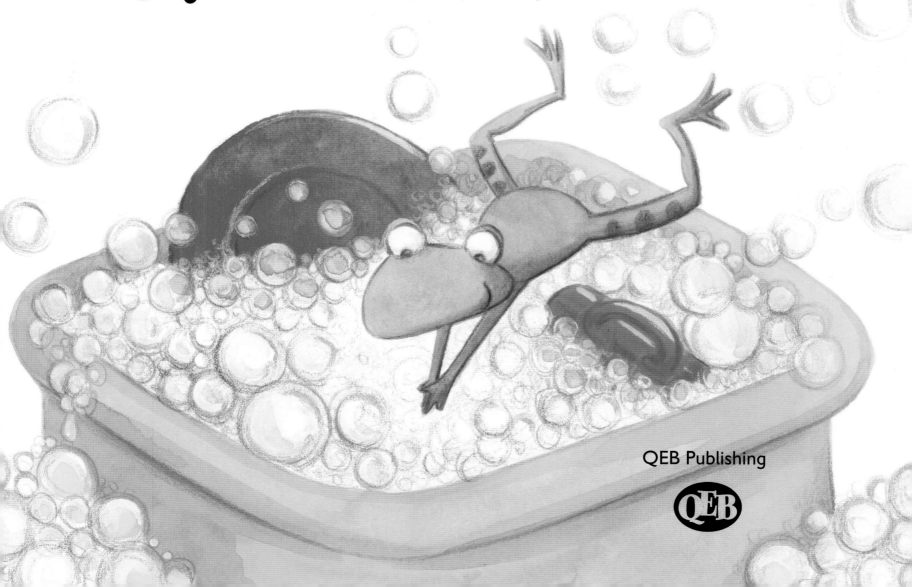

QEB Publishing

QEB

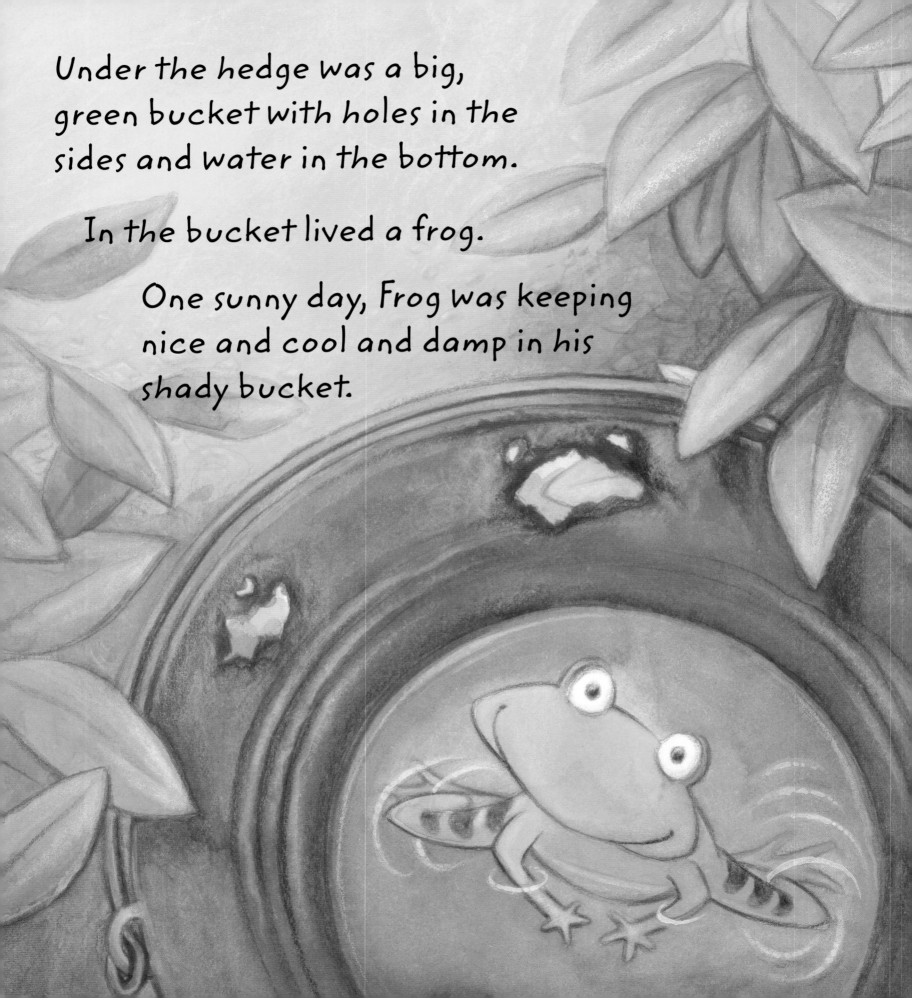

Under the hedge was a big, green bucket with holes in the sides and water in the bottom.

In the bucket lived a frog.

One sunny day, Frog was keeping nice and cool and damp in his shady bucket.

Then suddenly the bucket moved!

Frog saw a large hand holding the handle, and a **big voice** boomed:

This old thing will have to go!

"Then so will I!" croaked Frog, and off he hopped to find a new home.

It was a bad day to look for a new home.
The sun was shining and Frog felt hot.

He leaped into the rainwater barrel,
but it was empty.

He hopped toward a flowerpot, but someone already lived there.

"No frogs allowed in here!" squeaked Mouse. "You're too damp."

Frog hopped under a pile of leaves, but someone already lived there, too.

"No croakers in my house," grumbled Turtle. "You'll keep me awake."

Frog saw a cool, damp hole
under a tree, and looked in.

A little face
with bright eyes,
a pink nose, and long
whiskers popped up.

"No room in here,"
said Rabbit, wiggling her nose.
"There are ten of us already!"

Frog hopped over to a drainpipe.
Someone with eight long legs
climbed down to look at him.

"You can't come in here,"
said Spider.
"You'll make a mess of
my lovely web!"

Frog hopped away gloomily.
Nobody seemed to want him.

"Perhaps I'll find a home here," he said, as he jumped up a step,

hopped through a doorway, and into a kitchen.

PLOP! He dove into the soapy water, but he did not like the bubbles.

SPLASH!
He hopped into the water jug, but he did not like the ice cubes.

Frog gazed into the washing machine. His eyes popped as he watched the water **whizz** around and around.

"I don't want to be THAT clean!" said Frog.

Frog hopped upstairs and into the bathroom.
"Oooh! Lots of places here," he croaked.

He leaped into the sink,

but there was no water in it.

Then Frog heard running water.

He looked around and saw
water pouring into an
enormous bathtub.

In he hopped.

Ouch!

"Too hot for me!"
he croaked.

Frog hopped downstairs and out of the house.
The sun was even hotter. Poor Frog's skin felt dry.

He scrambled down the hot
path toward the shed.

He'd never been so far before.

"Oh, for a cool new
home!" he cried.

He hopped into the shed for some shade. And there in a corner was a beautiful bucket with some water in the bottom.

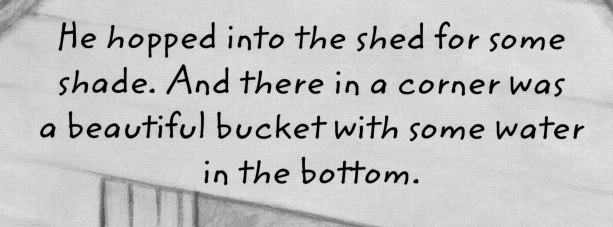

"It's just like my old one. Home, sweet home!" croaked Frog, as he jumped in with relief. The water felt lovely and cool on his skin.

Frog was so tired from all his hopping and searching that he fell fast asleep.

But he soon woke up when the bucket began to shake.

"Oh no, not again! I don't want to go anywhere," he croaked. "I've only just moved in!"

Frog slurped from side to side as the bucket
swung through the air. Then it stopped.
He scrambled up to the edge and peeped over.

"What very **big** boots!"
he croaked.

Frog and the water hurtled out of the bucket.

"It must be a dream... I am a flying frog!"
he croaked as he flew through
the air...

Frog swam to a large lily pad, pulled himself up and sat there, gazing around in wonder.

"I can't believe my luck," he said.
"This is the most beautiful home I have ever seen!"

Notes for parents and teachers

- Read the story to the children. Ask them to tell the story back to you. This is the beginning of reading. Later, help them to look for the word "Frog" on each page.

- Ask the children why Frog went looking for a new bucket, instead of looking for a pond or a lake. How do they think Frog felt when he was searching? What do they think happened to Frog when he went to live in the pond? Do they think he was happy in the end?

- Tell the children about tadpoles, (or polliwogs!) and the life cycle of the frog. Look for tadpoles in ponds, but leave them there to hatch. Get the children to go to the library and find a book with pictures that show the different changes the tadpole goes through before it becomes a frog. It's amazing!

- What kind of noise do the children think frogs make? Ribbit, ribbit... croak, croak... Have a competition for the best frog noise.

- Get the children to crouch down like a frog—get those knees bending!—and hop, hop, hop, making froggy jumps:
    Froggy jump high
    Froggy jump low
    All croak together and off we go!

- Help the children to make a beautiful picture of Frog's final pond. They could paint or crayon the water and stick on lily pads and flowers made of tissue paper. Trace a frog shape and let them cut out card or paper frogs and color them in. They can make Frog's eyes from bubble wrap. Draw or cut out dragonflies. Their lovely wings could be made from tissue paper, too.

- Frogs are funny, harmless, little creatures. Encourage the children to respect different creatures, however odd they look, and teach them not to harm things.

- Discuss with the children how frogs help the planet.

- Read more Frog stories to the children. There is the famous "The Tale of Mr. Jeremy Fisher" by Beatrix Potter and the delightful Frog and Toad books by Arnold Lobel.

- Creatures like Frog that live on land and in water are called amphibians. Can the children think of any other amphibians? There are salamanders and toads, for example.

- How many different kinds of frog do the children think there are in the world? Look for them together in books—there are frogs in rain forests, rivers, and ponds all over the world and some of them are beautiful. Talk about the importance of keeping them safe.

- Talk about different homes with the children and why they are important.